Learn ລາວ

Lao

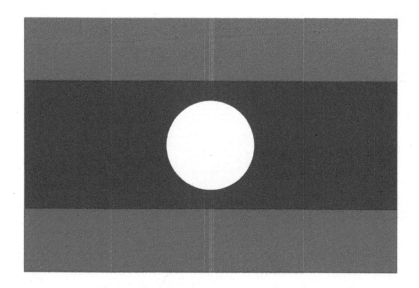

for beginners

Christopher Panaretos
ISBN 9798379019792

Table of Contents

Tips for Language Learning

The most important thing is **self-esteem**. You must have self esteem above a certain threshold, otherwise your brain will prevent you from learning. You won't be aware of this effect, you will simply not feel motivated to learn.

Secondly, **practice** speaking, listening, writing, and reading for yourself. You only get better at something when you actually do it, not by reading or listening to someone describe how to do something.

Lastly, **time**. You should achieve a basic beginner level after about 250 hours. At 500 hours, have a solid beginner understanding. And at 1000 hours get to an intermediate level.

Summary of Lao

Universal Grammar Rules

The explanation of Lao presented in this book is based on an alternative, universal theory of grammar that is much different from traditional grammar, although there is overlap with some concepts. However, this alternative grammar theory is concise and provides a solid foundation for understanding how language works in general, so it is a good base for Lao-specific language rules to stand on.

The alternative grammar theory has five main concepts: thing, descriptor, scene, thing-converter, and scene-converter.

- **thing**: there are 6 categories of things in the world
    - object
    - concept
    - time
    - place
    - process
    - state

- **descriptor**: each of the six kinds of things can have its own properties unique to that thing, like color, size, or speed

- scene: a scene is a relative arrangement of things, where one of the things acts as a verb, another acts as subject, and 0, 1, or 2 other things are included depending on the type of scene; there are four types of scene
    - linking
    - intransitive
    - monotransitive
    - ditransitive

- **thing-converter**: these words turn a particular type of thing into one of the other six types of things, or into a descriptor

- scene-converter: these words turn a scene into a thing or into a descriptor

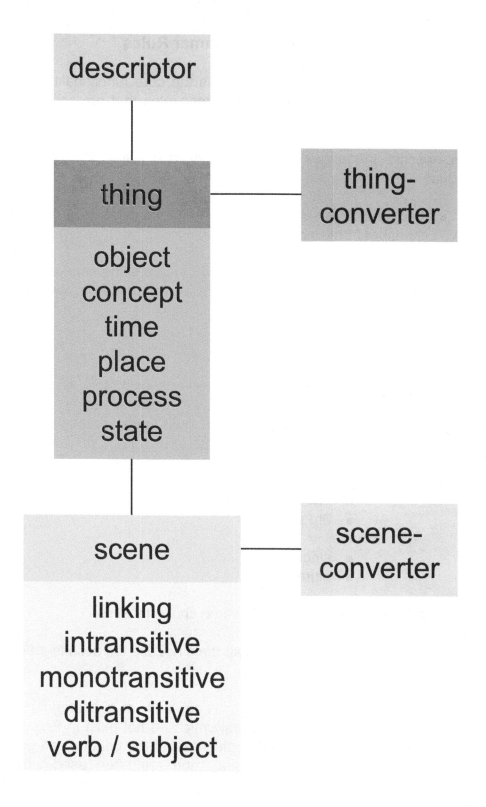

Lao-Specific Grammar Rules

The grammar system above describes the core functionality of all languages. It does not include grammar rules that are specific to individual languages.

Lao-specific languages rules that are discussed in this book include:

- **Lao alphabet** → Lao uses the Lao alphabet, not the Latin alphabet from English

- **tonal pronunciation** → meaning of words depends not only on the spelling of the word, but also the manner in which it is pronounced

- **case** → Lao does not use cases

- **things::personal pronouns** → a subcategory of things, pronouns are placeholders that point to other things; personal pronouns in particular point to people; Lao personal pronouns have two characteristics...
  - perspective
    - 1st person
    - 2nd person
    - 3rd person
  - count
    - singular
    - plural

- **things** → in Lao, things have no characteristics...

- **descriptors::articles** → Lao does not use the definite article or the indefinite article

- **descriptors::classifiers** → Lao has a subcategory of descriptors called classifiers, which do not exist in English; classifier words give information about the general category or some feature of a thing, and are often used when counting things

- **descriptors** → descriptors do not change spelling to match their target thing

- verbs → in Lao, verbs have three characteristics...
  - mood
    - indicative
    - subjunctive
    - imperative
  - tense
    - past
    - present
    - future
  - aspect
    - imperfect
    - perfect

Diagram of Lao-Specific Grammar Rules

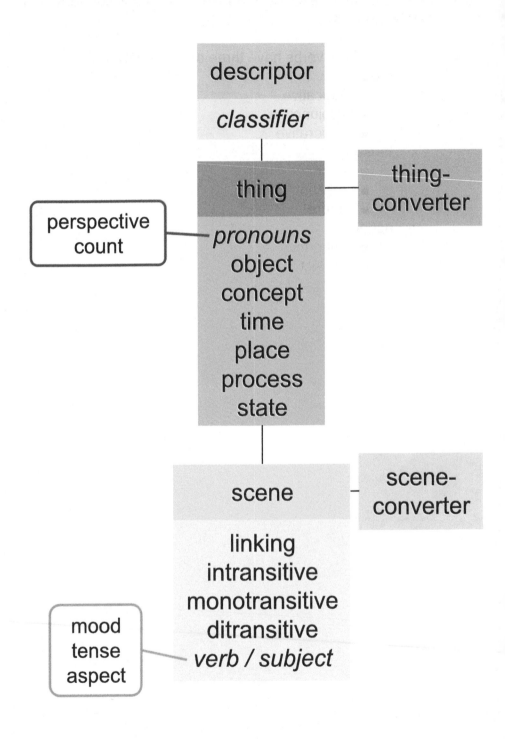

Spelling and Word Order

The grammar rules for Lao, as for all languages, can only be expressed in two fundamental ways: the spelling of each word, and the relative order of words. So for Lao, the question is how do the universal rules and the Lao-specific grammar rules manifest with respect to spelling and word order? Exploring this topic will be the focus of the rest of this book, but a summary is given here.

Spelling

- **personal pronouns** change spelling depending on their *perspective* and *count*

- **things** do not change spelling

- **definite article** does not exist

- **indefinite article** does not exist

- **descriptors** do not change spelling

- **verbs** themselves don't change spelling for *mood*, *tense*, *aspect*, but these characteristics can be indicated by the addition of *auxiliary verbs*

Word Order

- **descriptors** are placed *after* their target thing

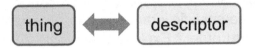

- **thing-converters** are placed *before* the target thing and the target thing's descriptors

- there are four types of scene, and each type has a different complement of things; however, all four types have a thing that acts as the scene's verb, and a thing that acts as the scene's subject; in general, Lao scenes start with the subject, then the verb follows immediately afterwards

linking

intransitive

monotransitive

ditransitive

- **scene-converters** are placed *before* their target scene

Consonants

T	ຕ	ຫ
K	ຄ	ຂ
S	ຊ	ສ
P	ພ	ພ
F	ຟ	ຝ
L	ລ	ຣ
H	ຣ	ຫ
Y	ຍ	ຢ
BP	ບ	

B	ບ
DT	ຕ
D	ດ
N	ນ
J	ຈ
G	ກ
W	ວ
M	ມ
NG	ງ

Vowels

ah	າ	-ະ	ັ
ai	ໄ	ໃ	
o	ໂ	ອ	
u	-ູ	-ຸ	
ee	-ີ	-ິ	
ue	-ື	-ຶ	
eh	ເ	ເ-ະ	
ae	ແ	ແ-ະ	
aw	ໍ	ເ-າະ	

euh	ငﬞ	ငﬞ
euh	ငﬞဒ	ငﬞဒ
ia	င-ဧ	ငﬞဧ
wa	ﬞဒ	ﬞဒး
ao	ငﬞၣ	
am	ၣ	

Syllable Units

Vowels can appear above, below, before, or after a consonant character. This results in **syllable units**, where the initial spoken consonant is often not written as the first character in the syllable unit.

ຂ້ອຍ

ຂ ອ ຍ

k o y

koy

i

ໄປ

ປ ໄ

b ai

bai

go

ກິນ

ກ ິ ນ

g i n

gin

to eat

ໂຍນ

ຍ ໂ ນ

y o n

yon

to throw

ເບສບໍ

ບ ເ ສ ບ ໍ

b ae s b aw

baes-baw

baseball

ໝາກໂປມ

ໝາກ ປ ໂ ມ

m a k p oh m

mak-pohm

apple

ຫາດຊາຍ

ຫ	າ	ດ		ຊ	າ	ຍ
h	ah	d		s	ah	y

had-sai

beach

ເບິ່ງ

ບ	ເ◌ິ່	ງ
b	euh	ng

beung

to watch

ການສະແດງ

ກ	າ	ນ		ສ	ະ		ດ	ແ	ງ
g	a	n		s	a		d	ae	ng

gan-sa-daeng

show

Scenes

What is a Scene

A scene is just a particular arrangement of things, where one of the things acts as a verb, and another as a subject.

The verb in a scene does not necessarily need to have a tense, it can be in an infinitive form or a continuous form.

Additionally, a scene can serve multiple purposes. It can serve as a complete sentence, standing on its own. It can also act as a thing or a descriptor, often with the help of a scene-converter word.

There are too many variations of scenes to show them all, but several will be demonstrated in this chapter.

Linking Scene as Sentence, has Tensed Verb

The Lao version of the sentence 'She is happy' is:

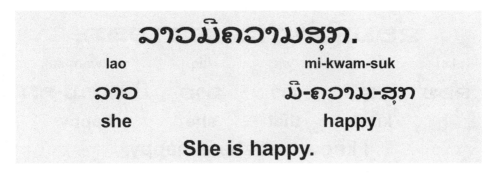

The subject 'ລາວ' is first, followed by the linking scene complement 'ມີຄວາມສຸກ'. In the Lao version, the linking verb 'to be' is implied, and not explicitly written.

This is a graphical diagram of the sentence. The Lao words are in the middle, in solid yellow. The names of the components for this linking scene, i.e. subject, verb, and complement, are shown above, in yellow outline. The universal categories of each word is given below; things are red font, and the descriptor is blue font.

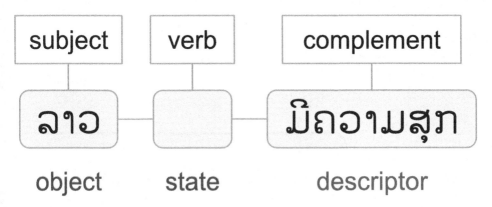

Linking Scene as a Thing, with Tensed Verb

The Lao version of the sentence 'I know that she is happy' is:

ຂ້ອຍ	ຮູ້	ວ່າ	ລາວ	ມີ-ຄວາມ-ສຸກ
koi	ru	wa	lao	mi-kwam-suk
ຂ້ອຍ	ຮູ້	ວ່າ	ລາວ	ມີ-ຄວາມ-ສຸກ
i	know	that	she	happy

I know that she is happy.

In this sentence, there are two scenes. One scene is the linking scene 'she is happy'. The other scene is 'I know [something]', which is a monotransitive scene. The linking scene is nested within the monotransitive scene.

Note that the inner linking scene is preceded by the scene-converter word 'that', which helps to indicate that the linking scene is going to be used as a thing within an enclosing scene.

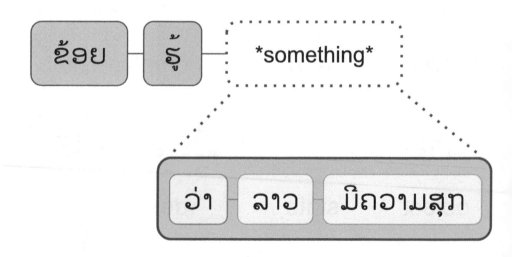

Intransitive Scene as Sentence, Converted Thing as Descriptor

The Lao version of the sentence 'The man swam in the lake' is:

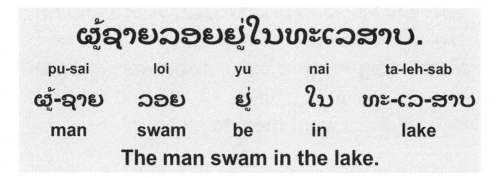

The simplest version of this intransitive scene is 'The man swam'. However, the example sentence also has a thing-converter word, 'in', to convert an object, 'the lake', into a location. Hence the phrase 'in the lake' is called a converted thing. Here, the phrase 'in the lake' is acting as a descriptor of the process 'swam', which is the verb of the intransitive scene.

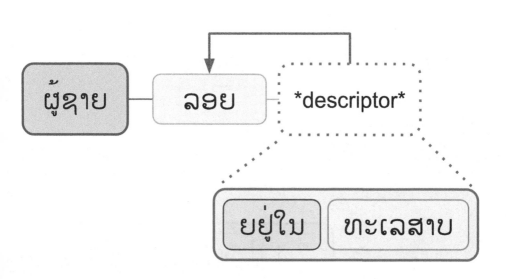

Intransitive Scene as Thing, with Untensed Verb

The Lao version of the sentence 'I want them to sleep' is:

ຂ້ອຍຕ້ອງການໃຫ້ພວກເຂົານອນ.

koi	tong-gan	hai	pwk-lao	non
ຂ້ອຍ	ຕ້ອງ-ການ	ໃຫ້	ພວກ-ເຂົາ	ນອນ
i	want	give	them	sleep

I want them to sleep.

The intransitive scene in this example is the nested 'them to sleep'. The outer scene 'i want [something]' is a monotransitive scene.

The Lao version is very different from English, it would be read literally as 'I want to give them sleep'. The nested scene 'them to sleep' is replaced with 'to give them sleep', which is an incomplete scene missing its subject: '[someone] to give them sleep'. The incomplete scene is being used as a thing, and it serves the role of direct object for the outer scene.

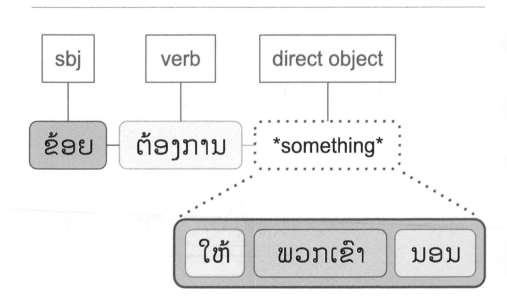

Monotransitive Scene as Sentence

The Lao version of the sentence 'I will order a pizza' is:

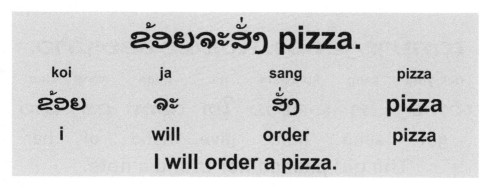

In this example, the scene is a sentence. It is a monotransitive scene, so there is a verb, subject, and direct object. The verb is 'to order' in the future tense, and in both English and Lao the future tense is indicated by the addition of an auxiliary verb, either 'will' or ຈະ.

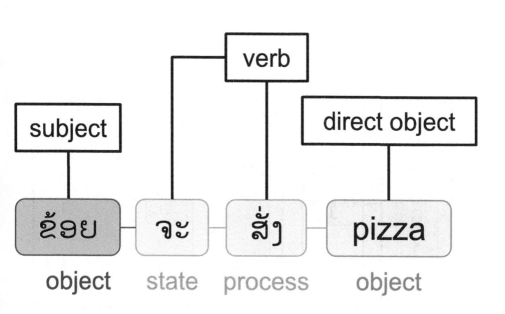

Ditransitive Scene as Sentence

The Lao version of the sentence 'The girl passed her friend a note' is:

ເດັກຍິງສົ່ງຂໍ້ຄວາມໃຫ້ເພື່ອນຂອງລາວ.

dek-ying	sang	ko-kwam	hai	puen	kong	lao
ເດັກ-ຍິງ	ສົ່ງ	ຂໍ້-ຄວາມ	ໃຫ້	ເພື່ອນ	ຂອງ	ລາວ
girl	send	note	give	friend	of	her

The girl passed her friend a note.

Here, the English ditransitive scene is translated into Lao as a monotransitive scene with a converted thing. The subject, verb, and direct object are directly translated. However, the indirect object 'her' is turned into 'to her friend', since the word 'give / ໃຫ້' could be thought of as the thing-converter 'to'.

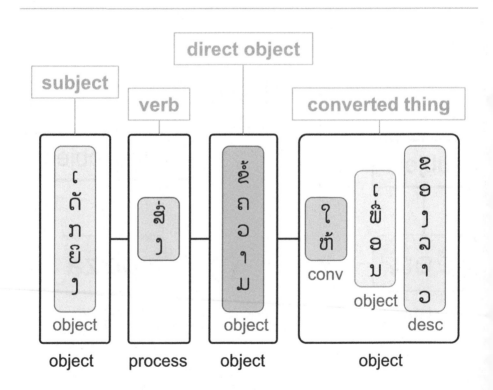

29

Personal Pronouns
as Subjects

ຂ້ອຍ	i
ພວກເຮົາ	we
ເຈົ້າ	you
ພວກເຈົ້າ	you all
ລາວ	he
ລາວ	she
ພວກເຂົາ	they

ຂ້ອຍເປັນຄົນຜູ້ໜຶ່ງ.

bpen	kon	pu	neung
ເປັນ	ຄົນ	ຜູ້	ໜຶ່ງ
am	person	*obj*	one

I am a person.

perspective	*count*	
1st	singular	ຂ້ອຍ
	plural	ພວກເຮົາ
2nd	singular	ເຈົ້າ
	plural	ພວກເຈົ້າ
3rd	singular	ລາວ
	plural	ພວກເຂົາ

ພວກເຂົາມິຄວາມສຸກ.

pwk-kao

ພວກ-ເຂົາ

they

mi-kwam-suk

ມິ-ຄວາມ-ສຸກ

happy

They are happy.

perspective	count	
1st	singular	ຂ້ອຍ
	plural	ພວກເຮົາ
2nd	singular	ເຈົ້າ
	plural	ພວກເຈົ້າ
3rd	singular	ລາວ
	plural	ພວກເຂົາ

ພວກເຮົາເບິ່ງໜັງ.

1st person, singular	

pwk-hao	beung	nang
ພວກ-ເຮົາ	ເບິ່ງ	ໜັງ
we	watched	movie

We watched a movie.

perspective	count	
1st	singular	ຂ້ອຍ
	plural	ພວກເຮົາ
2nd	singular	ເຈົ້າ
	plural	ພວກເຈົ້າ
3rd	singular	ລາວ
	plural	ພວກເຂົາ

ເຈົ້າກຳລັງເວົ້າ.

jao	kam-lang	wao
ເຈົ້າ	ກຳ-ລັງ	ເວົ້າ
you	-ing	talk

You are talking.

perspective	count	
1st	singular	ຂ້ອຍ
	plural	ພວກເຮົາ
2nd	singular	ເຈົ້າ
	plural	ພວກເຈົ້າ
3rd	singular	ລາວ
	plural	ພວກເຂົາ

Personal Pronouns
as Direct Objects

ຂ້ອຍ	i
ພວກເຮົາ	we
ເຈົ້າ	you
ພວກເຈົ້າ	you all
ລາວ	he
ລາວ	she
ພວກເຂົາ	they

ຂ້ອຍເຫັນເຈົ້າ.

koi	hen	2nd person, singular
		jao
ຂ້ອຍ	ເຫັນ	ເຈົ້າ
i	see	you

I see you.

perspective	count	
1st	singular	ຂ້ອຍ
	plural	ພວກເຮົາ
2nd	singular	ເຈົ້າ
	plural	ພວກເຈົ້າ
3rd	singular	ລາວ
	plural	ພວກເຂົາ

ເຈົ້າເອົາຂ້ອຍຂຶ້ນເຮືອ.

jao	ao	1st person, singular loi	kun	heu
ເຈົ້າ	ເອົາ	ຂ້ອຍ	ຂຶ້ນ	ເຮືອ
you	put	me	in	boat

You put **me** in the boat.

perspective	count		
1st	singular		ຂ້ອຍ
	plural		ພວກເຮົາ
2nd	singular		ເຈົ້າ
	plural		ພວກເຈົ້າ
3rd	singular		ລາວ
	plural		ພວກເຂົາ

ເຂົາເຈົ້າພາພວກເຮົາໄປຫໍສະໝຸດ.

kao	jao	pa	1st person, plural pwk-kao	bai	ho-sa-mut
ເຂົາ	ເຈົ້າ	ພາ	ພວກເຮົາ	ໄປ	ຫໍສະໝຸດ
him	you	lead	us	go	library

They take **us** to the library.

perspective	count	
1st	singular	ຂ້ອຍ
	plural	ພວກເຮົາ
2nd	singular	ເຈົ້າ
	plural	ພວກເຈົ້າ
3rd	singular	ລາວ
	plural	ພວກເຂົາ

ພວກເຮົາຍູ້ພວກເຂົາລົງນ້ຳ.

pwk-hao	yu	3rd person, plural pwk-kao	long	nam
ພວກເຮົາ	ຍູ້	ພວກເຂົາ	ລົງ	ນ້ຳ
we	push	them	down	water

We push **them** into the river.

perspective	count	
1st	singular	ຂ້ອຍ
	plural	ພວກເຮົາ
2nd	singular	ເຈົ້າ
	plural	ພວກເຈົ້າ
3rd	singular	ລາວ
	plural	ພວກເຂົາ

Personal Pronouns
as Indirect Objects

ຂ້ອຍ	i
ພວກເຮົາ	we
ເຈົ້າ	you
ພວກເຈົ້າ	you all
ລາວ	he
ລາວ	she
ພວກເຂົາ	they

ເຈົ້າເອົາປື້ມໃຫ້ຂ້ອຍ.

jao	ow	pum	hai	1st person, singular
				koi
ເຈົ້າ	ເອົາ	ປື້ມ	ໃຫ້	ຂ້ອຍ
you	take	book	give	me

You give me a book.

perspective	count	
1st	singular	ຂ້ອຍ
	plural	ພວກເຮົາ
2nd	singular	ເຈົ້າ
	plural	ພວກເຈົ້າ
3rd	singular	ລາວ
	plural	ພວກເຂົາ

ລາວໂຍນບານເບສບໍໃຫ້ລາວ.

					3rd person, singular
lao	yon	ban	baes-bo	hai	lao
ລາວ	ໂຍນ	ບານ	ເບສ-ບໍ	ໃຫ້	ລາວ
he	throws	ball	baseball	give	her

He throws **her** the baseball.

perspective	count	
1st	singular	ຂ້ອຍ
	plural	ພວກເຮົາ
2nd	singular	ເຈົ້າ
	plural	ພວກເຈົ້າ
3rd	singular	ລາວ
	plural	ພວກເຂົາ

ພວກເຮົາເອົາຮູບແຕ້ມໃຫ້**ະເຈົ້າ**ບ່ງ.

				3rd person, plural	
pwk-hao	ao	hub-taem	hai	ka-jao	beng
ພວກເຮົາ	ເອົາ	ຮູບແຕ້ມ	ໃຫ້	ະເຈົ້າ	ບ່ງ
we	show	painting	give	them	look

We show them a painting.

perspective	count	
1st	singular	ຂ້ອຍ
	plural	ພວກເຮົາ
2nd	singular	ເຈົ້າ
	plural	ພວກເຈົ້າ
3rd	singular	ລາວ
	plural	ພວກເຂົາ ະເຈົ້າ

ພວກເຂົາເອົາຮູບໃຫ້**ພວກເຮົາ**ເບິ່ງ.

pwk-kao	ao ·	rup	hai	**1st person, plural** pwk-hao	beng
ພວກເຂົາ	ເອົາ	ຮູບ	ໃຫ້	**ພວກເຮົາ**	ເບິ່ງ
they	take	photo	give	**us**	see

They show **us** the photograph.

perspective	*count*	
1st	singular	ຂ້ອຍ
	plural	**ພວກເຮົາ**
2nd	singular	ເຈົ້າ
	plural	ພວກເຈົ້າ
3rd	singular	ລາວ
	plural	ພວກເຂົາ

Things

Things in Lao have no characteristics. A thing's count is indicated by context.

ເດັກນ້ອຍຫຼິ້ນຢູ່ຂ້າງນອກ.

dek-noi	rin	yu	kang-nok
ເດັກ-ນ້ອຍ	ຫຼິ້ນ	ຢູ່	ຂ້າງ-ນອກ
child	plays	be	outside

The **child** plays outside.

Child / ເດັກນ້ອຍ

ເດັກນ້ອຍ

ເດັກນ້ອຍກຳລັງນອນຫຼັບ.

dek-noi	gam-lang	non-hlab
ເດັກ-ນ້ອຍ	ກຳ-ລັງ	ນອນ-ຫຼັບ
children	-ing	sleeping

The **children** are sleeping.

Child / ເດັກນ້ອຍ

ເດັກນ້ອຍ

ໝາຢູ່ເທິງຕັ່ງ.

ma	yu	teng	tang
ໝາ	ຢູ່	ເທິງ	ຕັ່ງ
dog	is	on	chair

The **dog** is on the chair.

Dog / ໝາ

ໝາ

ໝາດື່ມນ້ຳ.

ma	deum	nam
ໝາ	ດື່ມ	ນ້ຳ
dogs	drink	water

The **dogs** drink water.

Dog / ໝາ

ໝາ

ລາວມີສ້ອມ ແລະ ມິດ.

lao	mi	som	lae	mid
ລາວ	ມີ	ສ້ອມ	ແລະ	ມິດ
she	has	fork	and	knife

She has a **fork** and a knife.

Fork / ສ້ອມ

ສ້ອມ

ພວກເຮົາມີສ້ອມສອງອັນ ແລະ ມິດສອງອັນ.

pwk-hao	mi	som	song	an
ພວກເຮົາ	ມີ	ສ້ອມ	ສອງ	ອັນ
we	have	fork	2	*obj*

lae	mid	song	an
ແລະ	ມິດ	ສອງ	ອັນ
and	knife	2	*obj*

We have two **forks** and two knives.

Fork / ສ້ອມ

ສ້ອມ

Definite Article

Lao does not use the definite article.

ຂ້ອຍເຫັນຜູ້ຊາຍ.

koi	hen	pu-sai
ຂ້ອຍ	ເຫັນ	ຜູ້-ຊາຍ
i	see	man

I see **the** man.

ຜູ້ຍິງກຳລັງຍ່າງ.

pu-ying	gam-lang	yang
ຜູ້-ຍິງ	ກຳ-ລັງ	ຍ່າງ
women	-ing	walk

The ladies are walking.

ລາວດື່ມນ້ຳຮ້ອນ.

lao	deum	nam	hon
ລາວ	ດື່ມ	ນ້ຳ	ຮ້ອນ
he	drinks	water	hot

He drinks **the** hot water.

ເດັກຊາຍກິນເຂົ້າທ່ຽງ.

dek-sai	gin	kao-tiang
ເດັກ-ຊາຍ	ກິນ	ເຂົ້າ-ທ່ຽງ
boys	eat	lunch

The boys eat lunch.

ລາວປູກດອກໄມ້ຢູ່ໃນສວນ.

lao	puk	dok-mai	yu	nai	swn
ລາວ	ປູກ	ດອກ-ໄມ້	ຢູ່	ໃນ	ສວນ
he	planted	flowers	be	in	garden

He planted flowers in the garden.

ເຮືອນເປັນຂອງເຈົ້າ.

heuon	pen	kong	jao
ເຮືອນ	ເປັນ	ຂອງ	ເຈົ້າ
house	is	of	you

The house is yours.

Indefinite Article

The indefinite article is not used either.

ຂ້ອຍກິນໝາກໂປມ.

koi	gin	hmak-pom
ຂ້ອຍ	ກິນ	ໝາກ-ໂປມ
i	ate	apple

I ate **an** apple.

ພວກເຮົານັ່ງຢູ່ເກົ້າຕັ່ງ.

pwk-hao	nang	yu	toeng	tang
ພວກ-ເຮົາ	ນັ່ງ	ຢູ່	ເກົ້າ	ຕັ່ງ
we	sat	be	on	chairs

We sat on some chairs.

ພວກເຂົານອນຢູ່ໃນໂຮງແຮມ.

pwk-kao	non	yu-nai	hong-haem
ພວກ-ເຂົາ	ນອນ	ຢູ່-ໃນ	ໂຮງ-ແຮມ
they	sleep	in	hotel

They sleep in **a** hotel.

ລາວນຸ່ງເສື້ອເຊີດ.

lao	nung	seua-seud
ລາວ	ນຸ່ງ	ເສື້ອ-ເຊີດ
he	wears	shirt

He is wearing **a** shirt.

ລາວໄດ້ຊື້ຍົບໃຫມ່.

lao	dai	su	yan	hmai
ລາວ	ໄດ້	ຊື້	ຍົບ	ໃຫມ່
she	had	bought	airplane	new

She bought **a** new airplane.

ແມວກຳລັງນອນຢູ່ເທິງໂຊຟາ.

maew	gam-lang	non	yu	teung	so-fa
ແມວ	ກຳ-ລັງ	ນອນ	ຢູ່	ເທິງ	ໂຊ-ຟາ
cat	-ing	sleep	is	on	sofa

A cat is sleeping on the sofa.

Descriptors for

objects
concepts
times
places

As a Linking Scene Complement

When a descriptor is used in the complement slot of a linking scene, it does not change spelling to match the scene's subject.

As an Immediate Attribute to a Thing

When not placed in the complement position of a linking scene, descriptors are used as immediate neighbors to things. When used in this manner, they go after their target, and they do not change spelling to match the target.

Sometimes, an object classifier word is added in between a thing and its descriptor. There are dozens of object classifier words, used depending on the size, shape, and type of object that the thing is. For example, living animals would use a different object classifier than a pencil.

When used, the word order with object classifiers is generally:

- thing → classifier → descriptor
- house → *obj* → large
- cat → *obj* → quiet
- pencil → *obj* → expensive

ເຮືອນຫຼັງໃຫຍ່ຢູ່ເທິງພູ.

thing	classifier	descriptor			
heuon	lang	hyai	yu	teung	pu
ເຮືອນ	ຫຼັງ	ໃຫຍ່	ຢູ່	ເທິງ	ພູ
house	*obj*	big	is	on	hill

The **big** house is on the hill.

Big
ໃຫຍ່

ຂ້ອຍຊື້ຫມວກໃບໃໝ່.

		thing	classifier	descriptor
koi	seu	mwk	bai	mai
ຂ້ອຍ	ຊື້	ຫມວກ	ໃບ	ໃໝ່
i	bought	hat	*obj*	new

I bought a **new** hat.

New
ໃໝ່

ມັນເປັນການດີ.

		thing	descriptor
man	pen	kan	di
ມັນ	ເປັນ	ການ	ດີ
it	is	thing	good

It is good.

Good
ດີ

ພວກເຮົາຟັງເພັງສຽງດັງ.

		thing	descriptor
pwk-hao	fang	peng-siang	dang
ພວກ-ເຮົາ	ຟັງ	ເພັງ-ສຽງ	ດັງ
we	listen	music	loud

We listen to **loud** music.

Loud
ດັງ

ຂ້ອຍຊື້ເຮືອນຫຼັງໃຫຍ່.

		thing	classifier	descriptor
koi	su	heuon	lang	hyai
ຂ້ອຍ	ຊື້	ເຮືອນ	ຫຼັງ	ໃຫຍ່
i	bought	house	*obj*	big

I bought a **big** house.

Big

ໃຫຍ່

ສຽງເພງດັງມາຈາກວິທະຍຸ.

thing	descriptor			
siang-paeng	dang	ma	jak	wi-ta-yu
ສຽງ-ເພງ	ດັງ	ມາ	ຈາກ	ວິ-ທະ-ຍຸ
music	loud	comes	from	radio

The **loud** music is coming from the radio.

Loud

ດັງ

ລາວຈັບປານ້ອຍ.

		thing	descriptor
lao	jab	pba	noy
ລາວ	ຈັບ	ປາ	ນ້ອຍ
he	caught	fish	small

He caught a **small** fish.

Small

ນ້ອຍ

ຜູ້ໃຫຍ່ມີອາຍຸ.

thing		descriptor
pu-hyai	mi	ayu
ຜູ້-ໃຫຍ່	ມີ	ອາຍຸ
adults	have	age

Adults are **old**.

Age

ອາຍຸ

Descriptors for

processes
states

Not Used as a Linking Scene Complement

Descriptors for processes or states are usually not used as the complement item of a linking scene.

As an Immediate Attribute

It is much more common to use descriptors of processes and states in the attributive manner, regardless of whether or not their target is being used as the verb in a scene or as a thing.

ລາວແລ່ນຍ່າງໄວ.

	thing	descriptor	
lao	laen	yang	wai
ລາວ	ແລ່ນ	ຍ່າງ	ໄວ
she	run	like	fast

She runs **quickly**.

ລາວຫິວຕະຫຼອດ.

lao	hiw	descriptor ta-lod
ລາວ	ຫິວ	ຕະ-ຫຼອດ
he	hungry	always

He is **always** hungry.

ພວກເຮົາຮ້ອງເພງຍ່າງມີຄວາມສຸກ.

	thing	descriptor	
pwk-hao	hong-paeng	yang	mi-kwam-suk
ພວກ-ເຮົາ	ຮ້ອງ-ເພງ	ຍ່າງ	ມີ-ຄວາມ-ສຸກ
we	sing	like	happy

We sing happily.

Thing + Descriptor

Example Sentences

ແມວນ້ອຍໂດດ.

thing maew ແມວ cat	descriptor noi ນ້ອຍ little	dod ໂດດ jump

The small cat jumps.

ຊາຍສູງ, ຈ່ອຍດື່ມ.

thing sai ຊາຍ man	descriptor sung ສູງ tall	descriptor joi ຈ່ອຍ thin	deum ດື່ມ drinks

The tall, thin man drinks.

ງົວສີນ້ຳຕານນອນ.

thing ngua ງົວ cow	descriptor si-nam-tan ສີ-ນ້ຳ-ຕານ brown	non ນອນ sleeps

The brown cow sleeps.

ລາວເຫັນຍິງທີ່ສະຫຼາດຄົນໜຶ່ງ.

		thing		descriptor	classifier	descriptor
lao	hen	ying	tee	sa-lad	kon	neng
ລາວ	ເຫັນ	ຍິງ	ທີ່	ສະ-ຫຼາດ	ຄົນ	ໜຶ່ງ
he	sees	woman	that	smart	*obj*	one

He sees a smart woman.

ປາສີສົ້ມຂອງຂ້ອຍສີໂຕລອຍ.

thing	descriptor	possessive	descriptor	classifier	
ba	si-som	kong-koi	si	toh	loi
ປາ	ສີ-ສົ້ມ	ຂອງ-ຂ້ອຍ	ສີ່	ໂຕ	ລອຍ
fish	orange	my	four	*obj*	swim

My four orange fish swim.

ເຮືອນຄົວຂອງເຂົາເຈົ້າມີບ່ອງຍ້ຽມໃຫຍ່ຫຼາຍບ່ອງ.

	thing		possessive			thing
	heuon-kua		kong-lao-jao		mee	bong-yiam
	ເຮືອນ-ຄົວ		ຂອງ-ເຂົາ-ເຈົ້າ		ມີ	ບ່ອງ-ຍ້ຽມ
	kitchen		their		has	windows

descriptor	descriptor	classifier
yai	lai	bong
ໃຫຍ່	ຫຼາຍ	ບ່ອງ
big	many	*obj*

Their kitchen has many big windows.

ມີນົກນ້ອຍສີແດງສາມໂຕຢູ່ບ່ອນນີ້.

	thing	descriptor	descriptor	descriptor	classifier			
mi	nok	noi	si-daeng	sam	toh	yu	bon	ni
ມີ	ນົກ	ນ້ອຍ	ສີ-ແດງ	ສາມ	ໂຕ	ຢູ່	ບ່ອນ	ນີ້
have	bird	small	red	3	*obj*	is	place	this

There are **three small, red birds** here.

ຂ້ອຍຍາກກິນຄຸກກີ້ຫວານໆສິບອັນ.

			thing	descriptor	descriptor	classifier
koi	yak	gin	kuk-ki	hwan-hwan	sib	an
ຂ້ອຍ	ຍາກ	ກິນ	ຄຸກ-ກີ້	ຫວານ ໆ	ສິບ	ອັນ
i	want	eat	cookie	sweet	10	*obj*

I want to eat **ten sweet cookies**.

ບົ້ງສີນ້ຳຕານສິບສີ່ໂຕອາໃສຢູ່ພື້ນດິນ.

thing	descriptor	descriptor	classifier				
bang	nam-tan	sib-si	toh	a-sai	yu	teun	din
ບົ້ງ	ນ້ຳ-ຕານ	ສິບ-ສີ່	ໂຕ	ອາ-ໃສ	ຢູ່	ພື້ນ	ດິນ
worm	brown	14	*obj*	live	is	under	soil

Fourteen brown worms live underground.

Verbs

What are Verbs

Verbs are processes or states that are used in the verb slot of a scene. In Lao, verbs have mood, tense, and aspect.

Unlike English, Lao verbs do not change spelling to match their scene's subject.

Moods

There are three moods in Lao: indicative, subjunctive, and imperative.

- *Imperative* is used for giving commands.
- *Subjunctive* is to express a personal belief or opinion.
- *Indicative* is for making statements of facts or talking about things that are known as being true.

In this book, only the indicative is discussed, as it is the most commonly used mood.

Tense

There are three tenses in Lao: *past*, *present*, and *future*. These are self explanatory. Past tense is used to discuss things in the past, present tense for the present, and future tense for things that will happen in the future.

Aspect

There are two aspects: *imperfect / continuous* and *perfect*.

- *Imperfect* refers to processes or states that do not have a clear ending point, or have not ended yet.
- *Perfect* refers to processes or states that do have a clear ending point, or have already finished.

Spelling and Extra Words

Lao verbs recognize these three characteristics only by adding so-called auxiliary verbs, and not by changing their spelling.

Also, Lao verbs often use context to indicate tense. This means that a verb may be written in a simple present tense, but within the context of the sentence it is intended to refer to the past or future.

Lao verbs do not change spelling to match the subject...

ຂ້ອຍ ກິນ	i **eat**
ພວກເຮົາ ກິນ	we **eat**
ເຈົ້າ ກິນ	you **eat**
ເຈົ້າທຸກຄົນ ກິນ	you all **eat**
ລາວ ກິນ	he **eats**
ພວກເຂົາ ກິນ	they **eat**

...or for time. However, they do add auxiliary verbs.

Lao			i			
ຂ້ອຍ		ກິນ	i			**ate**
ຂ້ອຍ	ກຳລັງ	ກິນ	i		was	**eating**
ຂ້ອຍ		ກິນ ແລ້ວ	i	had		**eaten**
ຂ້ອຍ	ເຄີຍ	ກິນ	i	had	been	**eating**
ຂ້ອຍ		ກິນ	i			**eat**
ຂ້ອຍ	ກຳລັງ	ກິນ	i		am	**eating**
ຂ້ອຍ		ກິນ ແລ້ວ	i	have		**eaten**
ຂ້ອຍ	ໄດ້	ກິນ ແລ້ວ	i	have	been	**eating**
ຂ້ອຍ	ຈະ	ກິນ	i	will		**eat**
ຂ້ອຍ	ຈະ	ກິນ	i	will	be	**eating**
ຂ້ອຍ	ຈະໄດ້	ກິນ	i	will have		**eaten**
ຂ້ອຍ	ຈະໄດ້	ກິນ	i	will have been		**eating**

ຂ້ອຍໄປຮ້ານ.

	past imperfect by context	
koi	bai	han
ຂ້ອຍ	ໄປ	ຮ້ານ
i	went	store

I went to the store.

To Go / ໄປ

	aspect	aux	ໄປ	ແລ້ວ
past	imperfect			
	continuous	ກຳລັງ	ໄປ	
			ໄປ	ແລ້ວ
	perfect			
	continuous	ເຄີຍ	ໄປ	
present			ໄປ	
	imperfect			
	continuous	ກຳລັງ	ໄປ	
			ໄປ	ແລ້ວ
	perfect			
	continuous	ໄດ້	ໄປ	ແລ້ວ
future		ຈະ	ໄປ	
	imperfect			
	continuous	ຈະ	ໄປ	
		ຈະ ໄດ້	ໄປ	
	perfect			
	continuous	ຈະ ໄດ້	ໄປ	

ພວກເຂົາກຳລັງບິນ.

	continuous indicator	past imperfect by context
pwk-kao	gam-lang	bin
ພວກ-ເຂົາ	ກຳ-ລັງ	ບິນ
they	-ing	fly

They **were flying**.

To Fly / ບິນ

past	imperfect			ບິນ
		continuous	**ກຳລັງ**	**ບິນ**
	perfect			ບິນ	ແລ້ວ
		continuous	ເຄີຍ	ບິນ
present	imperfect			ບິນ
		continuous	ກຳລັງ	ບິນ
	perfect			ບິນ	ແລ້ວ
		continuous	ໄດ້	ບິນ	ແລ້ວ
future	imperfect		ຈະ	ບິນ
		continuous	ຈະ	ບິນ
	perfect		ຈະ ໄດ້	ບິນ
		continuous	ຈະ ໄດ້	ບິນ

ຂ້ອຍໄດ້ເວົ້າມື້ວານນີ້.

koi	indicates perfect aspect	past imperfect	meu-wan-ni
	dai	wao	
ຂ້ອຍ	ໄດ້	ເວົ້າ	ມື້-ວານ-ນີ້
i	had	spoke	yesterday

I **had spoken** yesterday.

To Speak / ເວົ້າ

	imperfect			ເວົ້າ
		continuous	ກຳລັງ	ເວົ້າ
past			ໄດ້	ເວົ້າ
	perfect			
		continuous	ເຄີຍ	ເວົ້າ
	imperfect			ເວົ້າ
		continuous	ກຳລັງ	ເວົ້າ
present				ເວົ້າ ແລ້ວ
	perfect			
		continuous	ໄດ້	ເວົ້າ ແລ້ວ
	imperfect		ຈະ	ເວົ້າ
		continuous	ຈະ	ເວົ້າ
future			ຈະ ໄດ້	ເວົ້າ
	perfect			
		continuous	ຈະ ໄດ້	ເວົ້າ

ລາວເຄີຍລອຍນ້ຳມາກ່ອນ.

koi	**keuy** (indicates past imperfect)	**loi-nam** (past imperfect)	ma	gon
ລາວ	**ເຄີຍ**	**ລອຍນ້ຳ**	ມາ	ກ່ອນ
i	used to	swim	come	before

She **had been swimming** before then.

To Swim / ລອຍນ້ຳ

past	imperfect			ລອຍນ້ຳ	
		continuous	ກຳລັງ	ລອຍນ້ຳ	
	perfect			ລອຍນ້ຳ	ແລ້ວ
		continuous	**ເຄີຍ**	**ລອຍນ້ຳ**	
present	imperfect			ລອຍນ້ຳ	
		continuous	ກຳລັງ	ລອຍນ້ຳ	
	perfect			ລອຍນ້ຳ	ແລ້ວ
		continuous	ໄດ້	ລອຍນ້ຳ	ແລ້ວ
future	imperfect		ຈະ	ລອຍນ້ຳ	
		continuous	ຈະ	ລອຍນ້ຳ	
	perfect		ຈະ ໄດ້	ລອຍນ້ຳ	
		continuous	ຈະ ໄດ້	ລອຍນ້ຳ	

ພວກເຮົາມີໝາຫ້າໂຕ.

pwk-hao	present imperfect mi	hma	ha	toh
ພວກ-ເຮົາ	ມີ	ໝາ	ຫ້າ	ໂຕ
we	have	dogs	5	*obj*

We have five dogs.

To Have / ມີ

past	imperfect		ມີ	
		continuous	ກຳລັງ	ມີ
	perfect		ມີ	ແລ້ວ
		continuous	ເຄີຍ	ມີ
present	imperfect		ມີ	
		continuous	ກຳລັງ	ມີ
	perfect		ມີ	ແລ້ວ
		continuous	ໄດ້	ມີ	ແລ້ວ
future	imperfect		ຈະ	ມີ
		continuous	ຈະ	ມີ
	perfect		ຈະ ໄດ້	ມີ
		continuous	ຈະ ໄດ້	ມີ

ເຈົ້າກຳລັງໂດດ.

	continuous indicator	present imperfect
jao	gam-lang	dohd
ເຈົ້າ	ກຳ-ລັງ	ໂດດ
you	-ing	jump

You are jumping.

To Jump / ໂດດ

	imperfect			ໂດດ
	continuous	ກຳລັງ	ໂດດ	
past				
	perfect		ໂດດ	ແລ້ວ
	continuous	ເຄີຍ	ໂດດ	
	imperfect			ໂດດ
	continuous	ກຳລັງ	ໂດດ	
present				
	perfect		ໂດດ	ແລ້ວ
	continuous	ໄດ້	ໂດດ	ແລ້ວ
	imperfect	ຈະ	ໂດດ	
	continuous	ຈະ	ໂດດ	
future				
	perfect	ຈະ ໄດ້	ໂດດ	
	continuous	ຈະ ໄດ້	ໂດດ	

ເຈົ້າໄດ້ຖາມຫຼາຍເທື່ອແລ້ວ.

jao	indicates perfect aspect	past imperfect	lai	teu	past tense indicator
	dai	tam			laew
ເຈົ້າ	ໄດ້	ຖາມ	ຫຼາຍ	ເທື່ອ	ແລ້ວ
you	have	asked	many	times	already

You **have asked** many times.

To Ask / ຖາມ

past	imperfect				ຖາມ
		continuous	ກຳລັງ	ຖາມ	
	perfect			ຖາມ	ແລ້ວ
		continuous	ເຄີຍ	ຖາມ	
present	imperfect				ຖາມ
		continuous	ກຳລັງ	ຖາມ	
	perfect		ໄດ້	ຖາມ	
		continuous	ໄດ້	ຖາມ	ແລ້ວ
future	imperfect		ຈະ	ຖາມ	
		continuous	ຈະ	ຖາມ	
	perfect		ຈະ ໄດ້	ຖາມ	
		continuous	ຈະ ໄດ້	ຖາມ	

81

ມື້ນີ້, ພວກເຮົາໄດ້ຫຼິ້ນເກມຄອມພິວເຕີ.

		indicate perfect aspect	present imperfect		
me-ni	pwk-hao	dai	len	gaem	com-piw-te
ມື້-ນີ້	ພວກເຮົາ	ໄດ້	ຫຼິ້ນ	ເກມ	ຄອມພິວເຕີ
today	we	have	play	game	computer

Today, we **have been playing** computer games.

To Play / ຫຼິ້ນ

past	imperfect			ຫຼິ້ນ	
		continuous	ກຳລັງ	ຫຼິ້ນ	
	perfect			ຫຼິ້ນ	ແລ້ວ
		continuous	ເຄີຍ	ຫຼິ້ນ	
present	imperfect			ຫຼິ້ນ	
		continuous	ກຳລັງ	ຫຼິ້ນ	
	perfect			ຫຼິ້ນ	ແລ້ວ
		continuous	ໄດ້	ຫຼິ້ນ	
future	imperfect		ຈະ	ຫຼິ້ນ	
		continuous	ຈະ	ຫຼິ້ນ	
	perfect		ຈະ ໄດ້	ຫຼິ້ນ	
		continuous	ຈະ ໄດ້	ຫຼິ້ນ	

ມື້ອື່ນ, ລາວຈະຂຽນເລື່ອງ.

mu-eun	lao	indicates future ja	present imperfect kian	leung
ມື້ອື່ນ	ລາວ	ຈະ	ຂຽນ	ເລື່ອງ
tomorrow	she	will	write	story

Tomorrow, she will write a story.

To Write / ຂຽນ

past	imperfect			ຂຽນ	
		continuous	ກຳລັງ	ຂຽນ	
	perfect			ຂຽນ	ແລ້ວ
		continuous	ເຄີຍ	ຂຽນ	
present	imperfect			ຂຽນ	
		continuous	ກຳລັງ	ຂຽນ	
	perfect			ຂຽນ	ແລ້ວ
		continuous	ໄດ້	ຂຽນ	ແລ້ວ
future	imperfect		ຈະ	ຂຽນ	
		continuous	ຈະ	ຂຽນ	
	perfect		ຈະ ໄດ້	ຂຽນ	
		continuous	ຈະ ໄດ້	ຂຽນ	

ພວກເຂົ້າຈະຮຽນ.

pwk-kao	indicates future	present imperfect
	ja	hian
ພວກ-ເຂົ້າ	ຈະ	ຮຽນ
they	will	study

They **will be studying**.

To Study / ຮຽນ

past	imperfect			ຮຽນ	
		continuous	ກຳລັງ	ຮຽນ	
	perfect			ຮຽນ	ແລ້ວ
		continuous	ເຄີຍ	ຮຽນ	
present	imperfect			ຮຽນ	
		continuous	ກຳລັງ	ຮຽນ	
	perfect			ຮຽນ	ແລ້ວ
		continuous	ໄດ້	ຮຽນ	ແລ້ວ
future	imperfect		ຈະ	ຮຽນ	
		continuous	ຈະ	ຮຽນ	
	perfect		ຈະ ໄດ້	ຮຽນ	
		continuous	ຈະ ໄດ້	ຮຽນ	

ຂ້ອຍລະກິນເຂົ້າທ່ຽງກ່ອນຂ້ອຍອອກໄປ.

koi	future ja	present imperfect gin	kao-tiang	gon	koi	oog-bai
ຂ້ອຍ	ລະ	ກິນ	ເຂົ້າ-ທ່ຽງ	ກ່ອນ	ຂ້ອຍ	ອອກ-ໄປ
i	will	eat	lunch	before	i	leave

I will have eaten lunch before I leave.

To Eat / ກິນ

past	imperfect			ກິນ	
		continuous	ກຳລັງ	ກິນ	
	perfect			ກິນ	ແລ້ວ
		continuous	ເຄີຍ	ກິນ	
present	imperfect			ກິນ	
		continuous	ກຳລັງ	ກິນ	
	perfect			ກິນ	ແລ້ວ
		continuous	ໄດ້	ກິນ	ແລ້ວ
future	imperfect		ລະ	ກິນ	
		continuous	ລະ	ກິນ	
	perfect		ລະ	ກິນ	
		continuous	ລະ ໄດ້	ກິນ	

85

ພວກເຂົາຈະລໍຖ້າເປັນເວລາຫນຶ່ງຊົ່ວໂມງ.

pwk-hao	future	present imperfect	pen	we-la	nung	sua-mong
	ja	lo-ta				
ພວກເຂົາ	ຈະ	ລໍ-ຖ້າ	ເປັນ	ເວ-ລາ	ຫນຶ່ງ	ຊົ່ວ-ໂມງ
they	will	wait	be	time	1	hour

They will have been waiting for an hour.

To Wait / ລໍຖ້າ

past	imperfect			ລໍຖ້າ	
		continuous	ກຳລັງ	ລໍຖ້າ	
	perfect			ລໍຖ້າ	ແລ້ວ
		continuous	ເຄີຍ	ລໍຖ້າ	
present	imperfect			ລໍຖ້າ	
		continuous	ກຳລັງ	ລໍຖ້າ	
	perfect			ລໍຖ້າ	ແລ້ວ
		continuous	ໄດ້	ລໍຖ້າ	ແລ້ວ
future	imperfect		ຈະ	ລໍຖ້າ	
		continuous	ຈະ	ລໍຖ້າ	
	perfect		ຈະ ໄດ້	ລໍຖ້າ	
		continuous	ຈະ	ລໍຖ້າ	

Thing-Converters

In Lao, thing-converters, also known as prepositions in traditional grammar, are placed before their target thing.

ຂ້ອຍໄປຮ້ານຂາຍເຄື່ອງ.

koi	bai	thing ran	hai-keung
ຂ້ອຍ	ໄປ	ຮ້ານ	ຂາຍ-ເຄື່ອງ
i	go	store	shopping

I go **to** the store.

ລາວຍ່າງອອກໜ້າລາວ.

lao	yang	thing-converter oog-na	thing lao
ລາວ	ຍ່າງ	ອອກ-ໜ້າ	ລາວ
she	walk	in front of	him

She walks **in front of** him.

ມັນຢູ່ໃນຖົງ.

man	yu	thing- converter nai	thing tong
ມັນ	ຢູ່	ໃນ	ຖົງ
it	is	in	bag

It is **in** the bag.

ນ້ຳສຳລັບໝາ.

	thing-converter	thing
nam	sam-lab	ma
ນ້ຳ	ສຳ-ລັບ	ໝາ
water	for	dog

The water is **for** the dog.

ປຶ້ມຢູ່ເທິງໂຕະ.

		thing-converter	thing
pum	yu	teng	toh
ປຶ້ມ	ຢູ່	ເທິງ	ໂຕະ
book	is	on	table

The book is **on** the desk.

ລາວໄປກັບລາວ.

		thing-converter	thing
lao	bai	gab	lao
ລາວ	ໄປ	ກັບ	ລາວ
he	go	with	her

He goes **with** her.

ເຈົ້າຢູ່ເຮືອນ.

jao	yu	thing heun
ເຈົ້າ	ຢູ່	ເຮືອນ
you	are	home

You are **at** home.

ຕັ່ງຢູ່ໄກ້ກັບຄອມພິວເຕີ.

tang	yu	thing-converter		thing
		gai	**gab**	com-piw-teu
ຕັ່ງ	ຢູ່	**ໄກ້**	**ກັບ**	ຄອມ-ພິວ-ເຕີ
chair	is	**near**	**with**	computer

The chair is **by** the computer.

ພວກເຮົາມາຈາກປະເທດລາວ.

pwk-hao	ma	thing-converter	thing	
		jak	pa-tet	lao
ພວກ-ເຮົາ	ມາ	**ຈາກ**	ປະ-ເທດ	ລາວ
we	come	**from**	country	Laos

We are **from** Laos.

ລິງຍ່າງຂຶ້ນຂັ້ນໃດ.

ling	yang	thing-converter keum	thing kam-dai
ລິງ	ຍ່າງ	ຂຶ້ນ	ຂັ້ນ-ໃດ
monkey	walk	**up**	stairs

The monkey walks **up** the stairs.

ໜັງເປັນໜັງກ່ຽວກັບອາຫານ.

nang	pen	nang	thing-converter giaw-gab	thing a-han
ໜັງ	ເປັນ	ໜັງ	ກ່ຽວ-ກັບ	ອາ-ຫານ
movie	is	movie	**about**	food

The movie is about food.

ໜູແລ່ນໃນໄປໃນເຂົາວົງກົດ.

nu	laen	thing-converter			thing
		nai	bai	nai	kao-wong-kod
ໜູ	ແລ່ນ	ໃນ	ໄປ	ໃນ	ເຂົາ-ວົງ-ກົດ
mouse	run	**in**	**go**	**in**	maze

The mouse runs **into** the maze.

ຍົນບິນຜ່ານພວກເຮົາໄປ.

yon	bin	thing-converter **pan**	thing pwk-hao	bai
ຍົນ	ບິນ	**ຜ່ານ**	ພວກ-ເຮົາ	ໄປ
airplane	fly	**pass**	us	go

The airplane flies **over** us.

ຂ້ອຍອອກໄປຫຼັງຈາກການສະແດງ.

koi	oog-bai	thing-converter **lang-jak**	thing gan-sa-daeng
ຂ້ອຍ	ອອກ-ໄປ	**ຫຼັງ-ຈາກ**	ການ-ສະ-ແດງ
i	leave	**after**	show

I leave **after** the show.

ປາຢູ່ກ້ອງເຮືອ.

ba	yu	thing-converter **kong**	thing heu
ປາ	ຢູ່	**ກ້ອງ**	ເຮືອ
fish	are	**under**	boat

The fish are **under** the boat.

Scene-Converters

Scene-Converters used with Complete Scenes

Scene-converters, also known as subordinating conjunctions in traditional grammar terminology, are placed before their target scene. In these examples, the scenes attached to the scene-converter are all complete, meaning they don't have any missing scene components.

Example #1

In this example, the scene 'she gave him a book' is being used as a thing, specifically a concept. It serves the role of a direct object in the outer scene, 'i thought [something]'.

ຂ້າພະເຈົ້າຄິດວ່ານາງໃຫ້ເຂົາເປັນຫນັງສື.

ka-pa-jao	kid	scene-converter wa	subject nang
ຂ້າ-ພະ-ເຈົ້າ	ຄິດ	ວ່າ	ນາງ
i	thought	**that**	she

verb hai	indirect object lao	pen	direct object hnang-se
ໃຫ້	ເຂົາ	ເປັນ	ຫນັງ-ສື
gave	him	is	book

I thought **that she gave him a book.**

Example #2

Here, the scene 'the train will leave' is also being used as a thing, specifically a time. It serves the role of direct object in the outer scene 'he knows [something]'.

ລາວຮູ້ວ່າເວລາໃດລົດໄຟຈະອອກ.

		scene-converter			subject	verb	
lao	ru	wa	we-la	dai	lod-fai	ja	oog
ລາວ	ຮູ້	ວ່າ	ເວ-ລາ	ໃດ	ລົດ-ໄຟ	ຈະ	ອອກ
he	knows	that	time	which	train	will	leave

He knows **when the train will leave**.

Example #3

The scene 'the treats were hidden' is used as a thing, specifically a place. It serves the role of direct object in the outer scene 'the dog discovered [something]'.

ຫມາຄົ້ນພົບບ່ອນທີ່ເຂົ້າຫນົມໄດ້ຖືກ
ເຊື່ອງໄວ້.

		scene-converter	subject		verb
hma	kan-pab	bon-ti	kao-nom	dai-tuk	seung-wai
ຫມາ	ຄົ້ນພົບ	ບ່ອນທີ່	ເຂົ້າຫນົມ	ໄດ້ຖືກ	ເຊື່ອງໄວ້
dog	discovered	where	treats	were	hidden

The dog discovered where the treats were hidden.

Scene-Converters used with Incomplete Scenes

Scene-converters can also be used with scenes that have a missing component. In this book, scenes with a missing component are referred to as blanked scenes. Blanked scenes are often used as descriptors of things.

Example #4

In this example, the blanked scene 'i read [ ]' is being used as a descriptor for its target thing, 'the book'.

The blanked scene is blanked because it is missing its direct object. If the target thing were written into the blanked scene, it would become the complete scene: 'i read the book'.

The entire target + descriptor unit, 'the book that i read', plays the role of a subject in the enclosing sentence: '[it] was interesting'.

ປຶ້ມທ່ີຂ້ອຍໄດ້ອ່ານແມ່ນໜ້າສົນໃຈ.

target	scene-converter	subject	verb			
pum	ti	koi	dai	ahn	maen	na-san-jai
ປຶ້ມ	ທ່ີ	ຂ້ອຍ	ໄດ້	ອ່ານ	ແມ່ນ	ໜ້າ-ສົນ-ໃຈ
book	that	i	had	read	indeed	interesting

The book that I read was interesting.

96

Example #5

Here, the blanked scene 'we made [ ]' is being used as a descriptor for its target thing, 'the salad'.

This blanked scene is blanked because it is missing its direct object. If the target were written into the blanked scene, it would become the complete scene: 'we made the salad'.

The entire target + descriptor unit 'the salad that we made' plays the role of a direct object in the enclosing sentence: 'he ate [it]'.

ລາວກິນສະຫຼັດທີ່ພວກເຮົາເຮັດ.

		target	scene-converter	subject	verb
lao	gin	sa-lad	**ti**	pwk-hao	hed
ລາວ	ກິນ	ສະ-ຫຼັດ	**ທີ່**	ພວກ-ເຮົາ	ເຮັດ
he	ate	salad	**that**	we	made

He ate **the salad that we made**.

Example #6

Here, the blanked scene 'she gave me [ ]' is being used as a descriptor for its target thing, 'the box'.

This blanked scene is blanked because it is missing its direct object. Written as a complete scene, the target + descriptor unit would be: 'she gave me the box'.

The entire target + descriptor unit 'the box that she gave me' plays the role of a subject in the enclosing scene: '[it] was green]'.

ກ່ອງທີ່ລາວໃຫ້ຂ້ອຍແມ່ນສີຂຽວ.

target	scene-converter	subject	verb
kong	**ti**	lao	hai
ກ່ອງ	**ທີ່**	ລາວ	ໃຫ້
box	**that**	she	gave

indirect object		
koi	maen	si-kiaw
ຂ້ອຍ	ແມ່ນ	ສີ-ຂຽວ
me	was	green

The box that she gave me was green.

Practice Sentences

ແມວສີເທົ່າແລ່ນມິດໆຢູ່ເທິງຮົ້ວ.

thing	descriptor	present	descriptor
maew	si-tao	laen	mid-mid
ແມວ	ສີ-ເທົ່າ	ແລ່ນ	ມິດ ໆ
cat	gray	run	quietly

	thing-converter		thing
yu	teng		how
ຢູ່	ເທິງ		ຮົ້ວ
at	on		fence

The gray cat runs quietly on the fence.

ຂ້ອຍກິນມັນຝະລັ່ງຫົວໃຫຍ່ໆຊ້າໆເປັນຫນຶ່ງຊົ່ວໂມງ.

1st, singular	present	thing	classifier	descriptor
koi	gin	man-fa-lang	hua	yai-yai
ຂ້ອຍ	ກິນ	ມັນ-ຝະ-ລັ່ງ	ຫົວ	ໃຫຍ່ ໆ
i	eat	potato	*obj*	big

descriptor	thing-converter	descriptor	thing
sa-sa	pen	neng	sua-mong
ຊ້າ ໆ	ເປັນ	ຫນຶ່ງ	ຊົ່ວ-ໂມງ
slowly	is	one	hour

I slowly eat large potatoes for one hour.

ລາວຊື້ຮູບແຕ້ມເກົ່າຫຼາຍຮູບຈາກຮ້ານ.

3rd, singular, feminine	present	thing	descriptor
lao	se	hup-taen	gao
ລາວ	ຊື້	ຮູບ-ແຕ້ມ	ເກົ່າ
she	buy	painting	old

descriptor	classifier	thing-converter	thing
rai	hup	jak	ran
ຫຼາຍ	ຮູບ	ຈາກ	ຮ້ານ
many	*obj*	from	store

She bought many old paintings from the store.

ຊາຍເຕ້ຍສິບຄົນໂດດຂ້າມຕັ່ງຢ່າງມ່ອນຊື່ນ.

thing	descriptor	descriptor	classifer
sai	tey	sib	kon
ຊາຍ	ເຕ້ຍ	ສິບ	ຄົນ
man	short	ten	*obj*

present	thing-converter	thing	descriptor
dod	kam	tang	yang-mwn-sen
ໂດດ	ຂ້າມ	ຕັ່ງ	ຢ່າງ-ມ່ອນ-ຊື່ນ
jump	over	chair	happily

The ten short men jump happily over the chair.

Scene Builder

1) Pick a scene type

    a) Scene comes with empty sockets for subject, verb, and maybe a complement or objects

    b) Pick a process or state to act as the scene's verb

2) Plug pronouns or things into the subject and object sockets

    a) Pronoun - choose its correct spelling based on its perspective and count

    b) Thing - only one spelling to choose from

        i) Descriptors - these do not change spelling to match their target

3) Decide the verb's mood, tense, and aspect

4) Choose correct spelling of the verb based on mood, tense, and aspect

I ate a large pizza.

1) [to eat] → ກິນ, **within monotransitive scene**
    a) ກິນ(SBJ, DO)

2) 2 sockets
    a) SBJ [i] → ຂ້ອຍ
        i)   Personal Pronoun
            (1)   Perspective: 1st person
            (2)   Count: singular

    b) DO [a large pizza]
        i)   Thing + Descriptors
            (1)   Thing: [pizza] → ພິຊຊ່າ
            (2)   Indefinite Article: [a] → **n/a**
            (3)   Adjective: [large] → ໃຫຍ່

3) Verb will have
    a) Mood: indicative
    b) Tense: past
    c) Aspect: imperfect

4) Choose spelling of ກິນ for MTA:
    a) MTA = indicative, past, imperfect
    b) ກິນ → ກິນ

5) Lao translation is: ກິນ(ຂ້ອຍ, ພິຊຊ່າ ໃຫຍ່)

ຂ້ອຍກິນພິຊຊ່າໃຫຍ່

Made in the USA
Las Vegas, NV
02 January 2024

83833977R00059